RED	Danger. Passion, Love, Fire
BLUE	Power, Dignity, Clarity
YELLOW	Energy, Lightness, Joy
GREEN	Nature, Green, Fertility
VIOLET	Wisdom Spirituality, Strength, Healing
Pink	Healthy, Romantic, Innocent
Orange	Flamboyance, Success

Coloring focuses your energy outside of yourself, makes a difference in the world around you.

Adding color, representative or disturbing, can be a way to restore harmony, or a harmless rebellion that releases stress.

Even if you don't think you are an artist, adding color to a black and white World IS art.

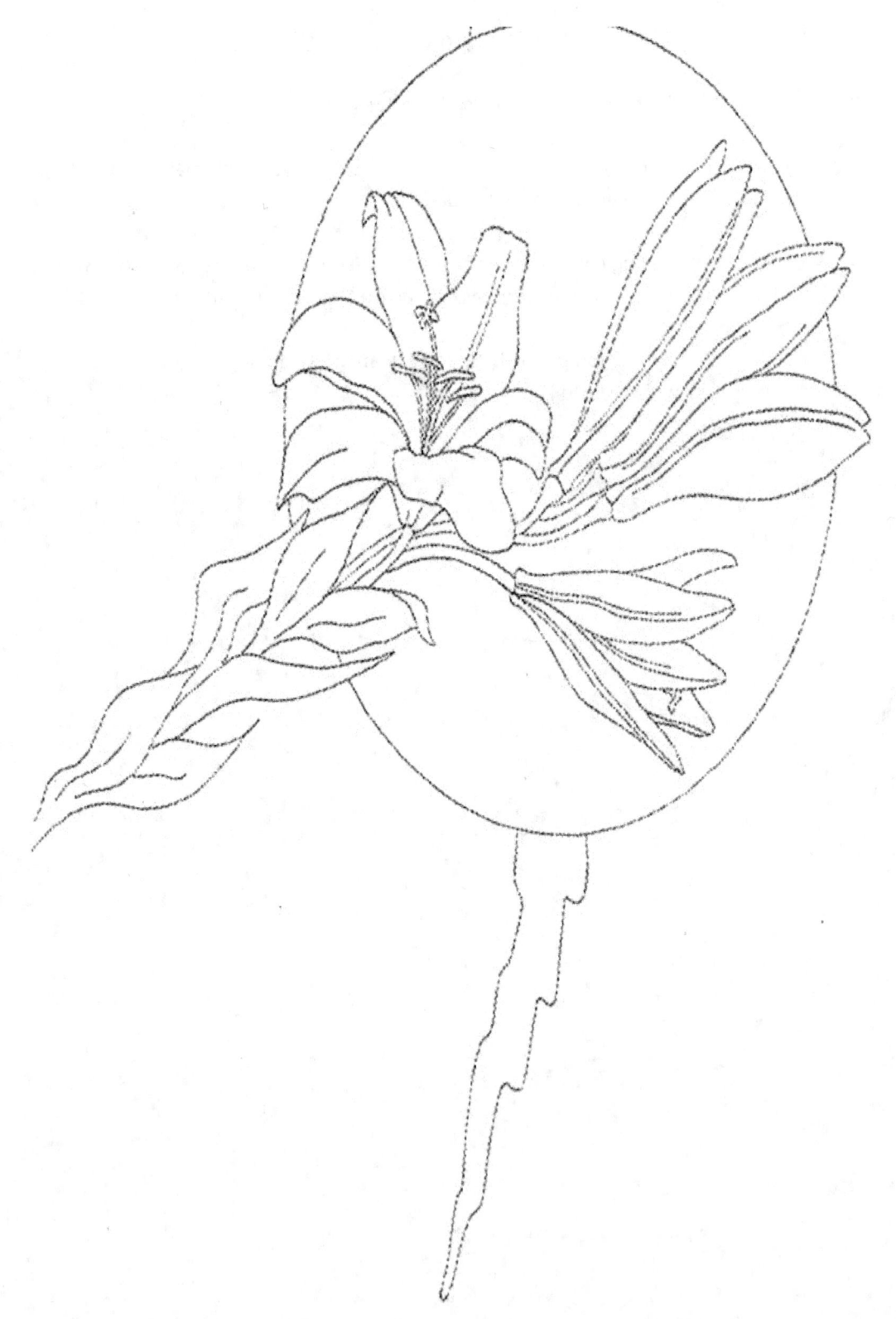

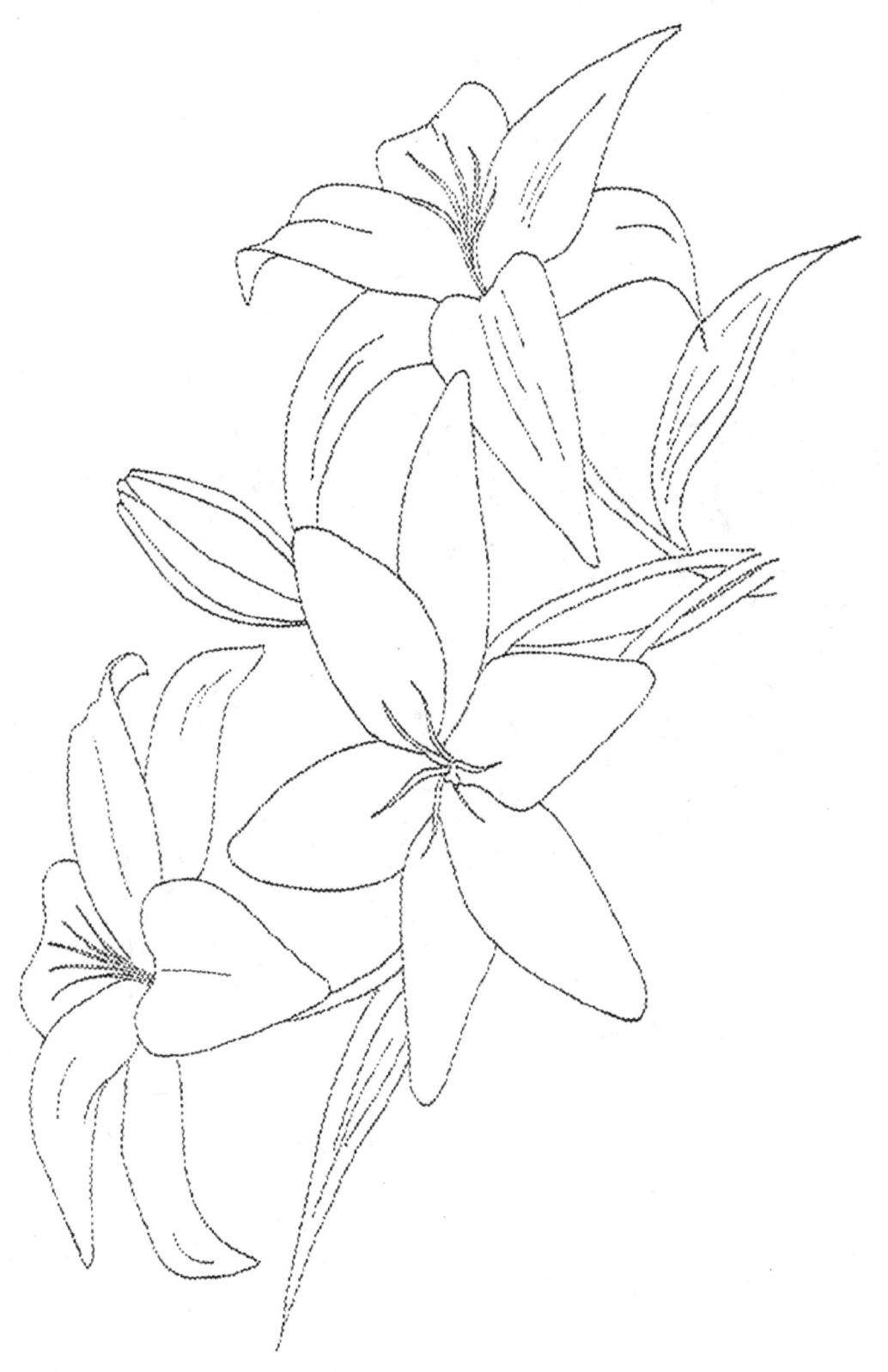

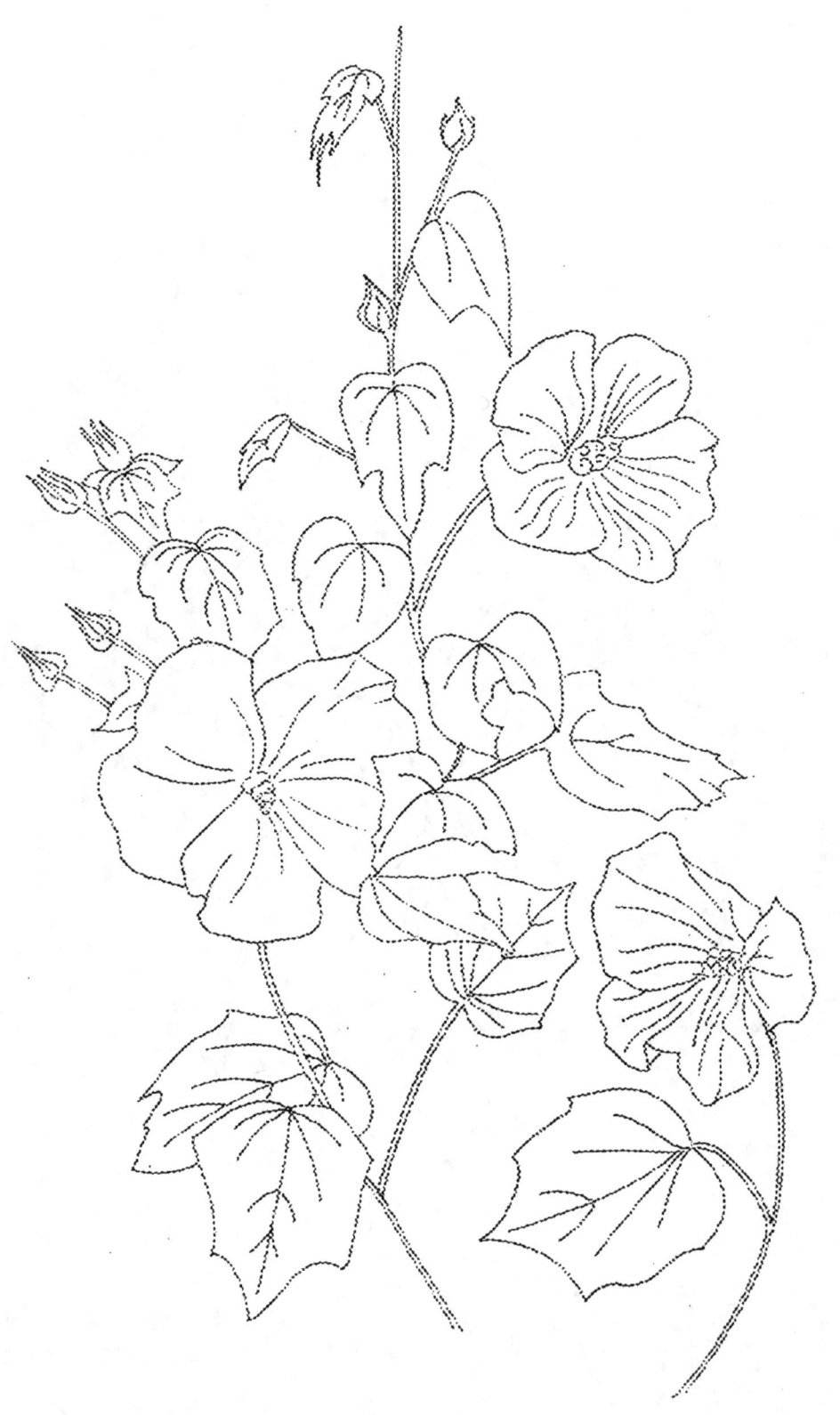

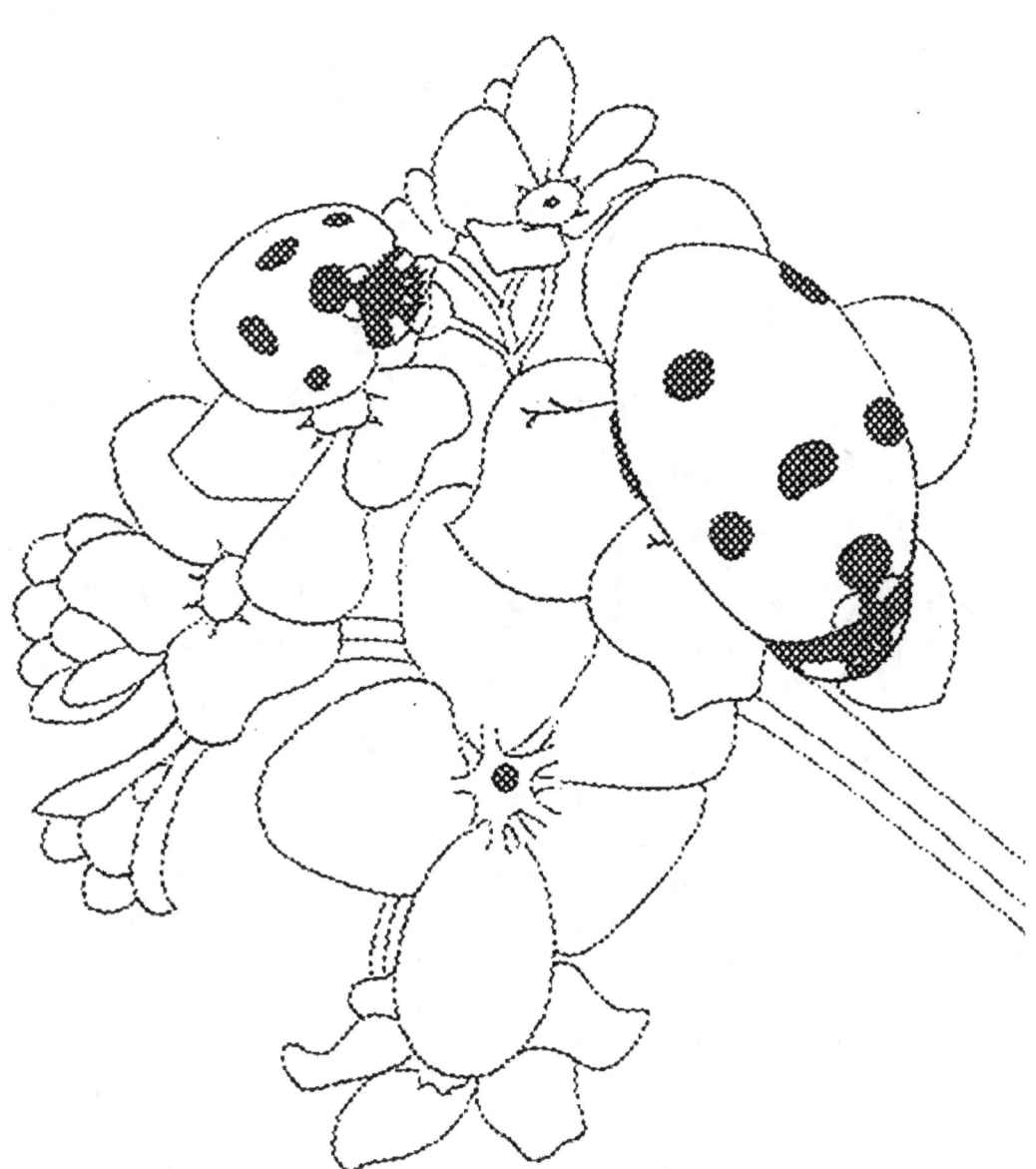

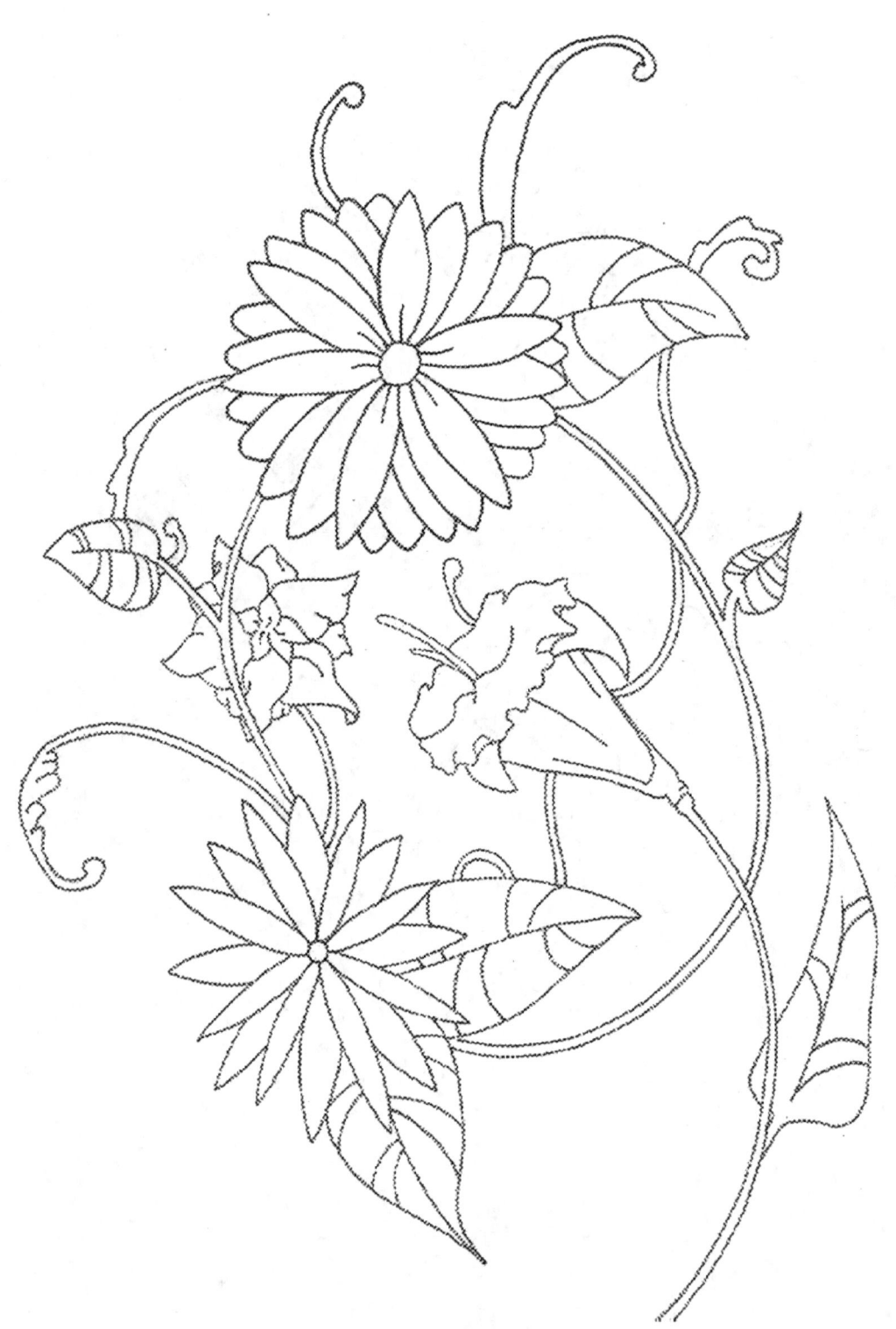

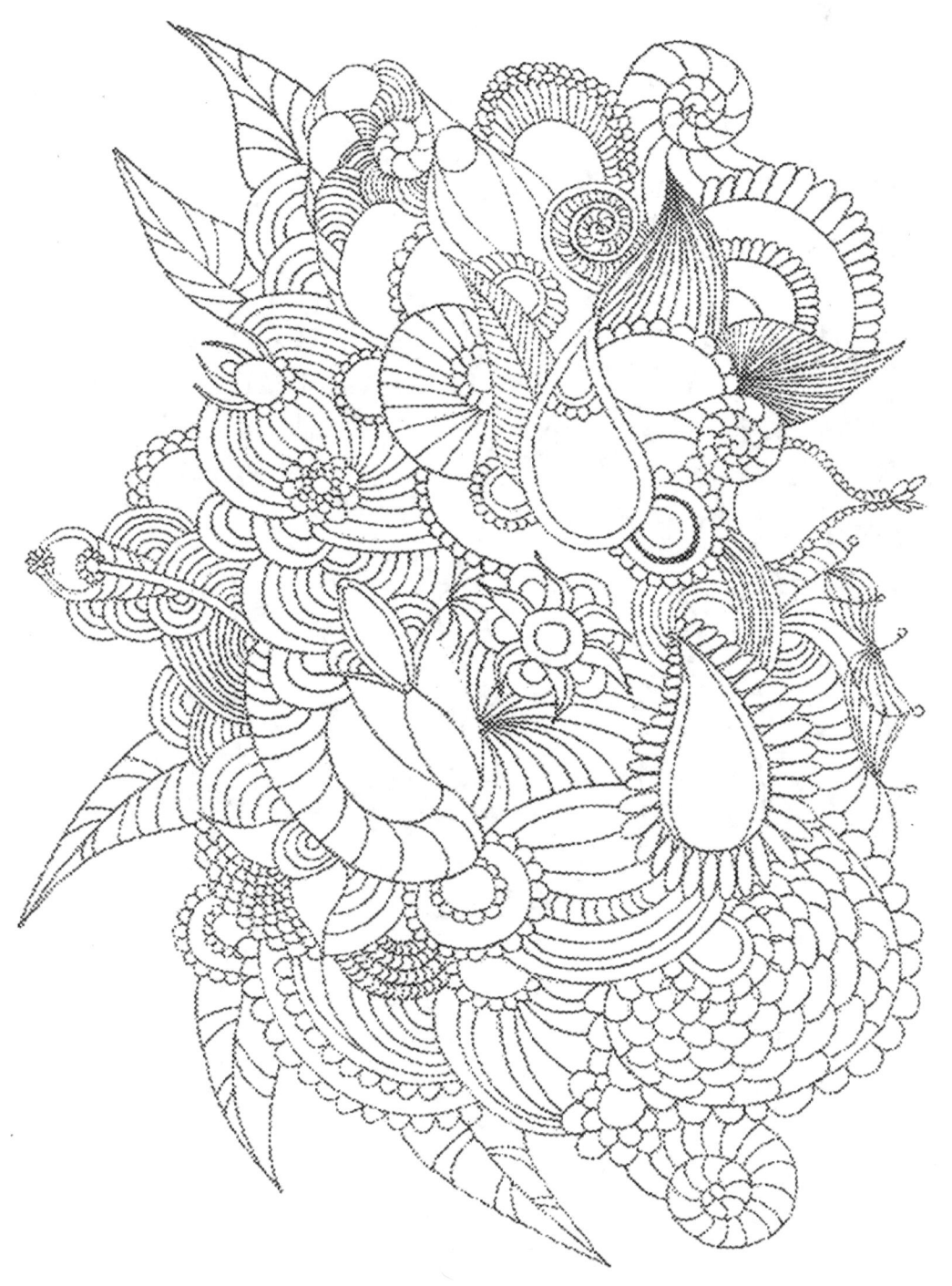

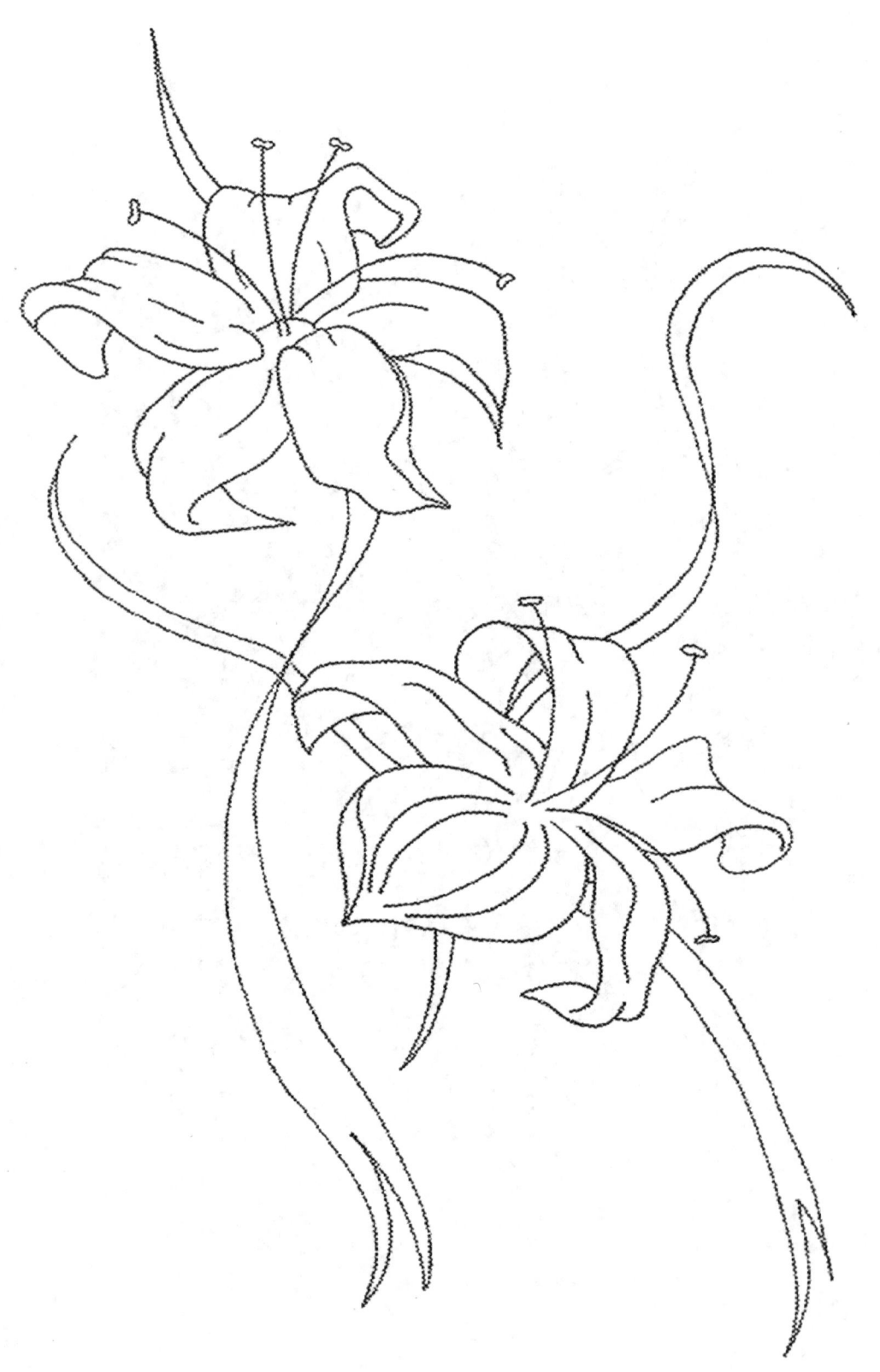

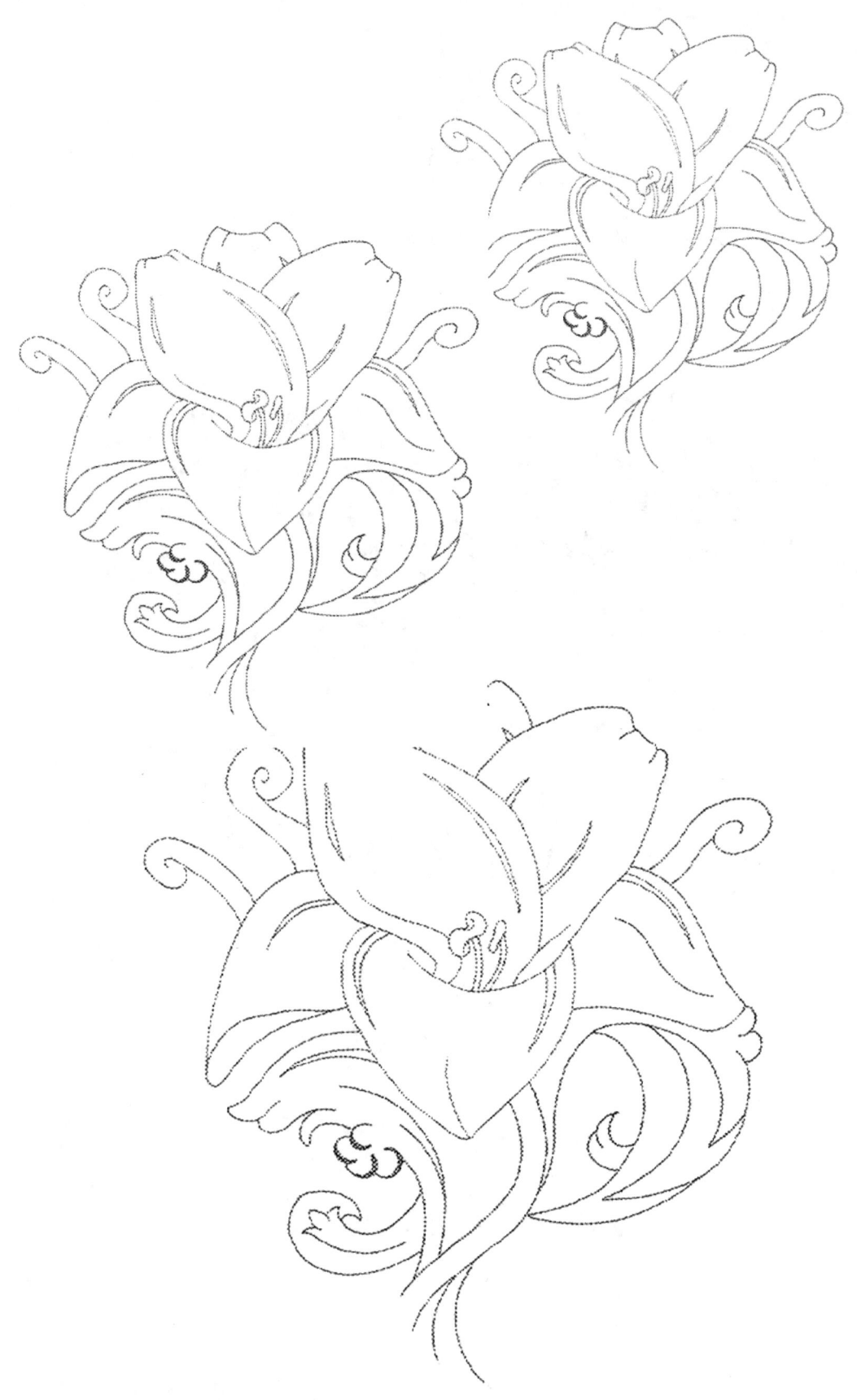

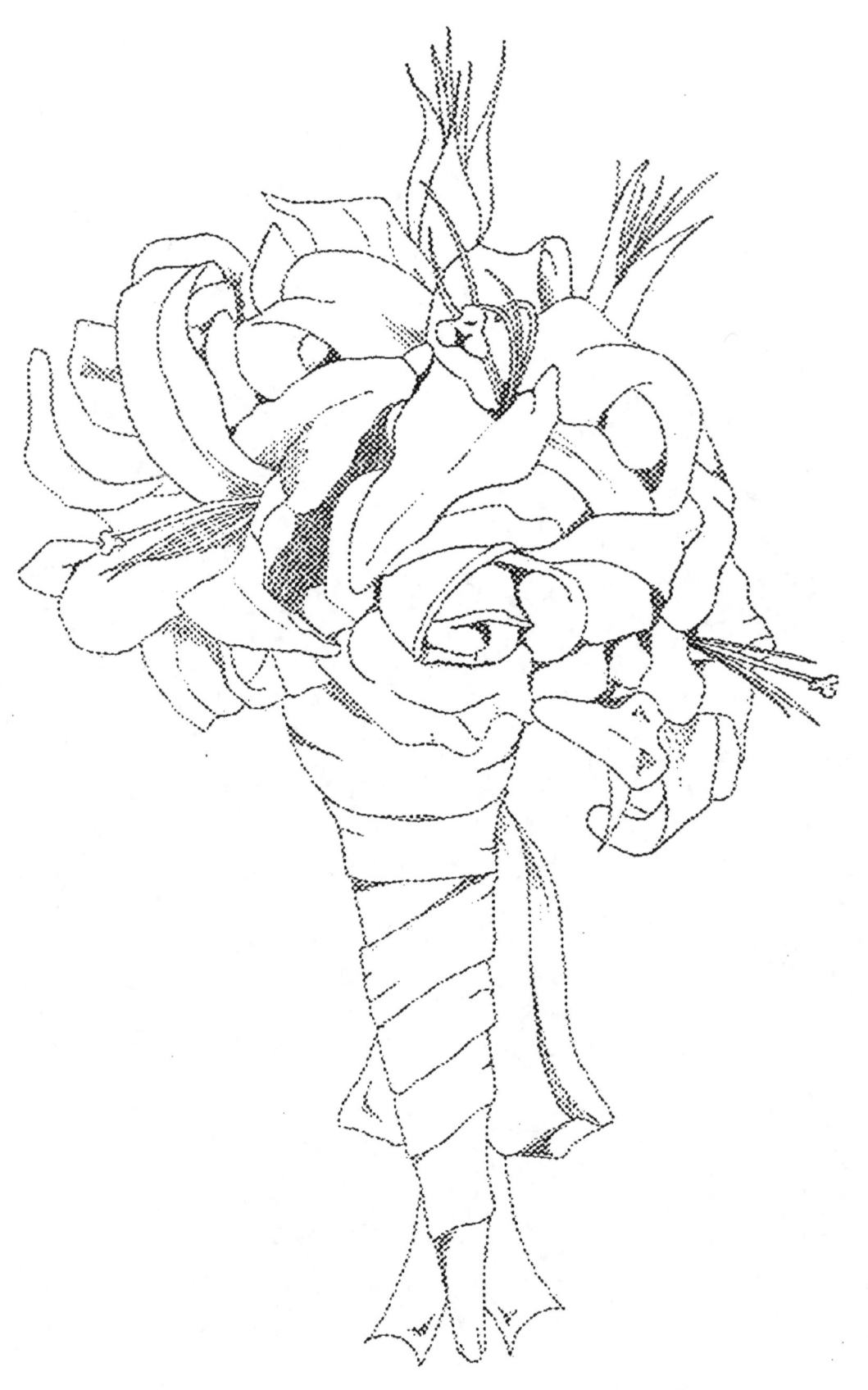

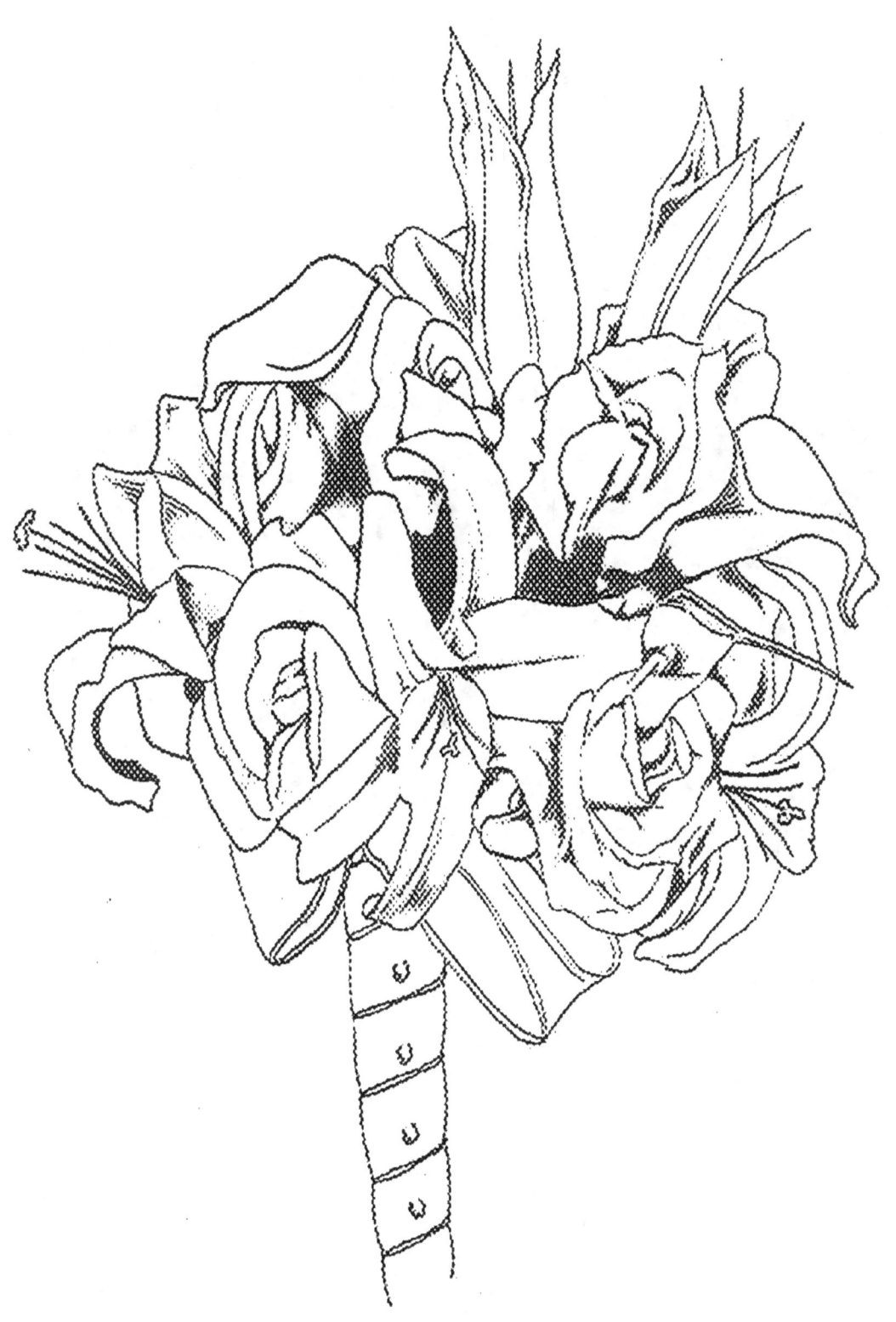

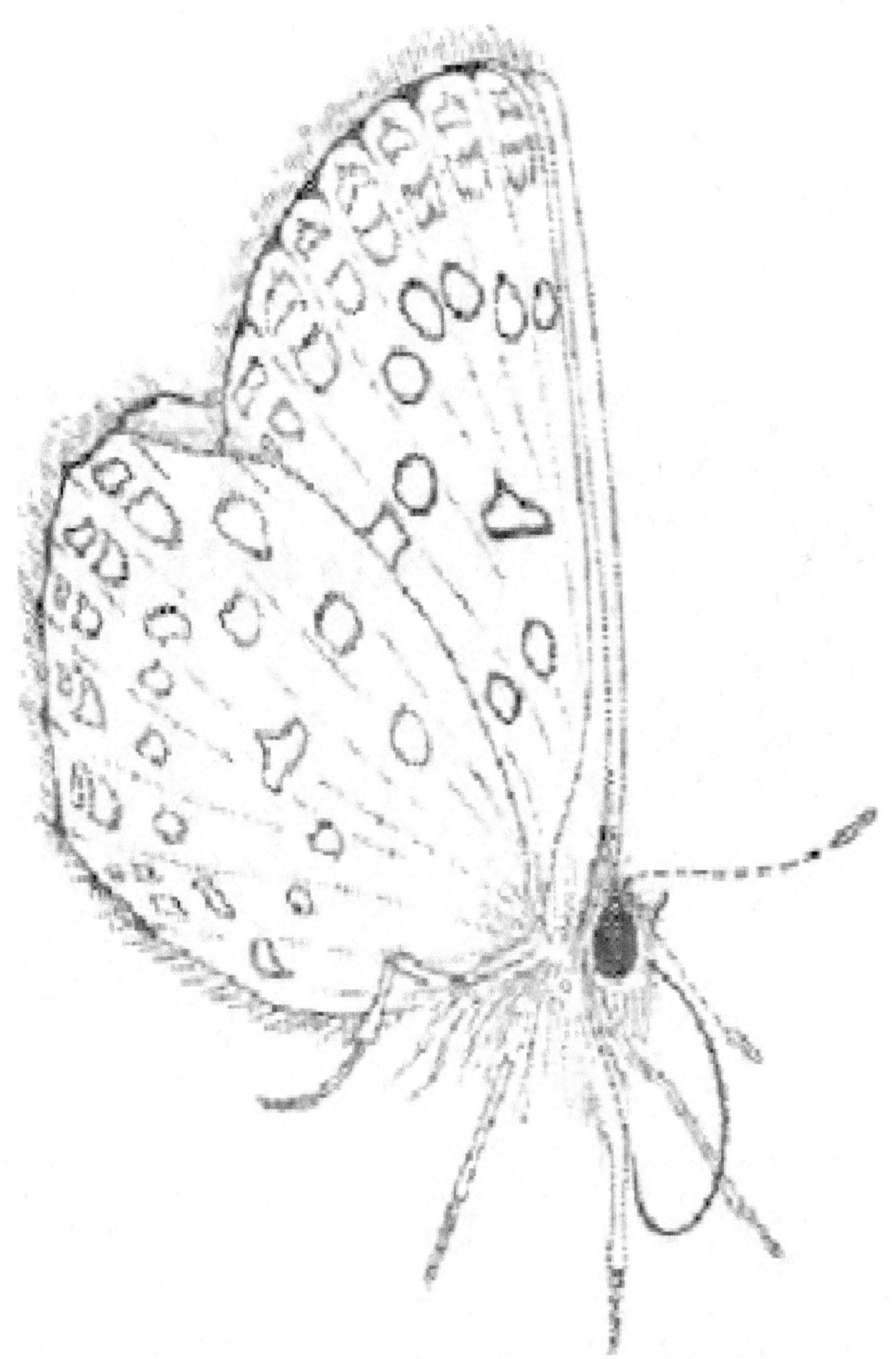

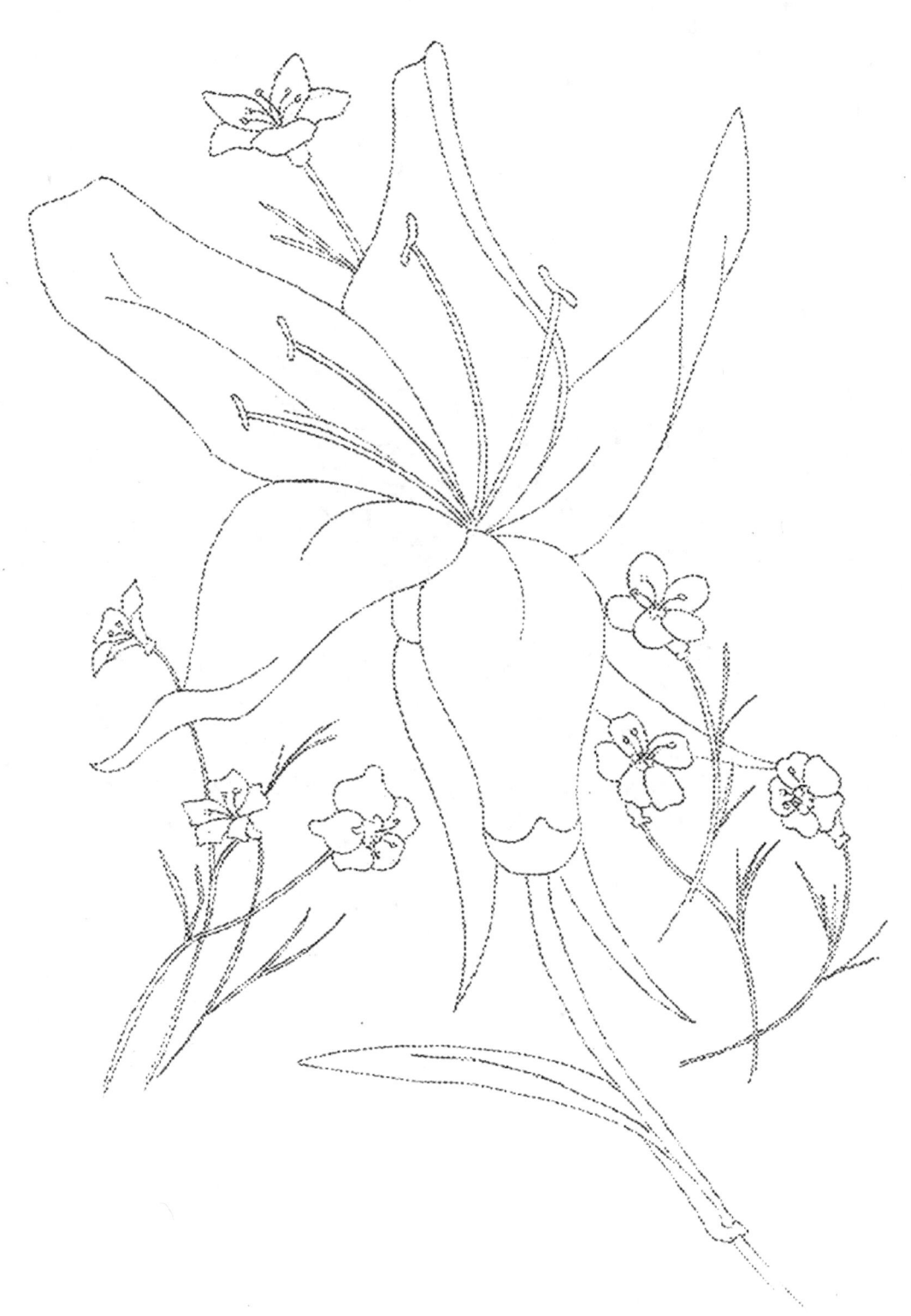

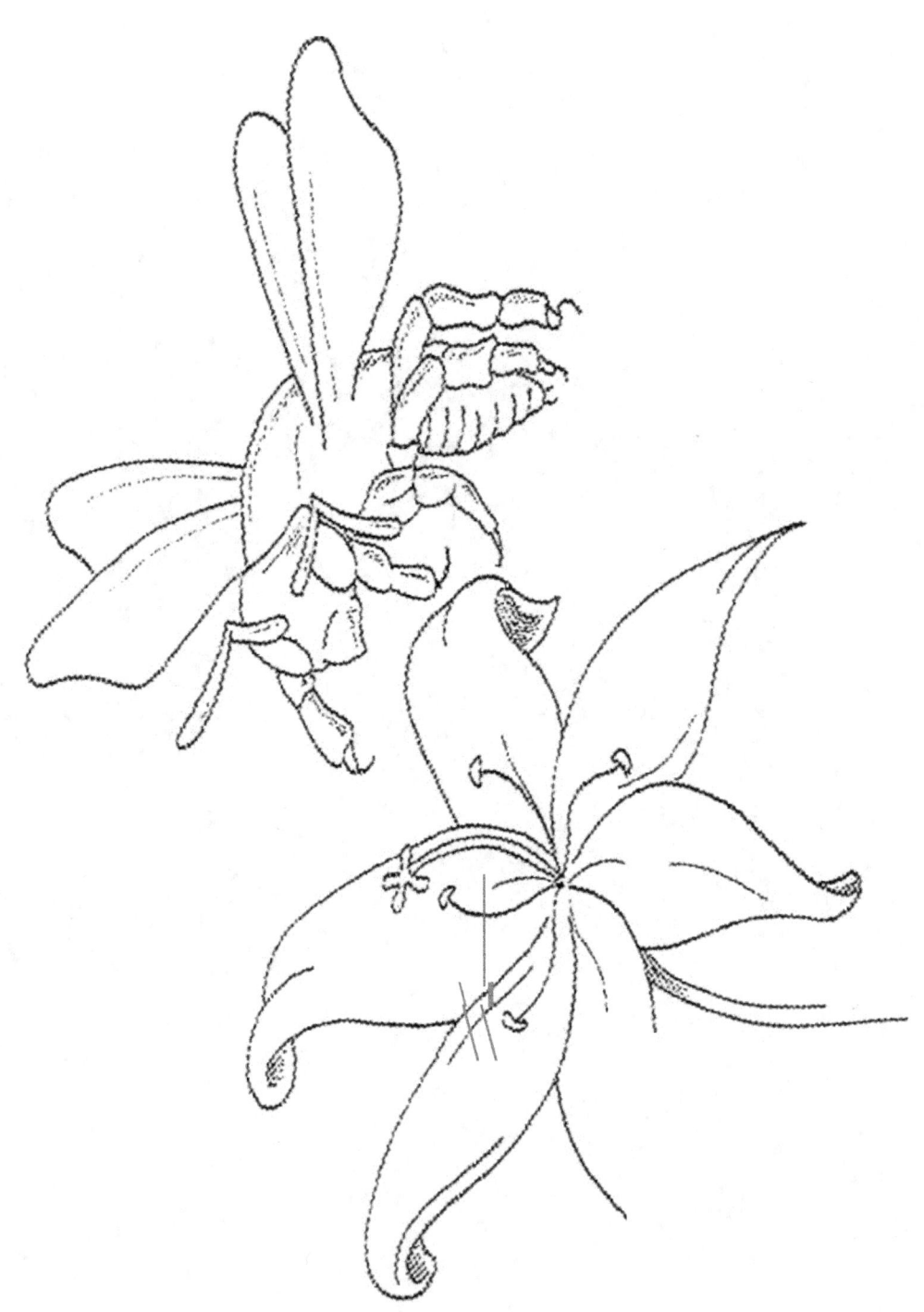

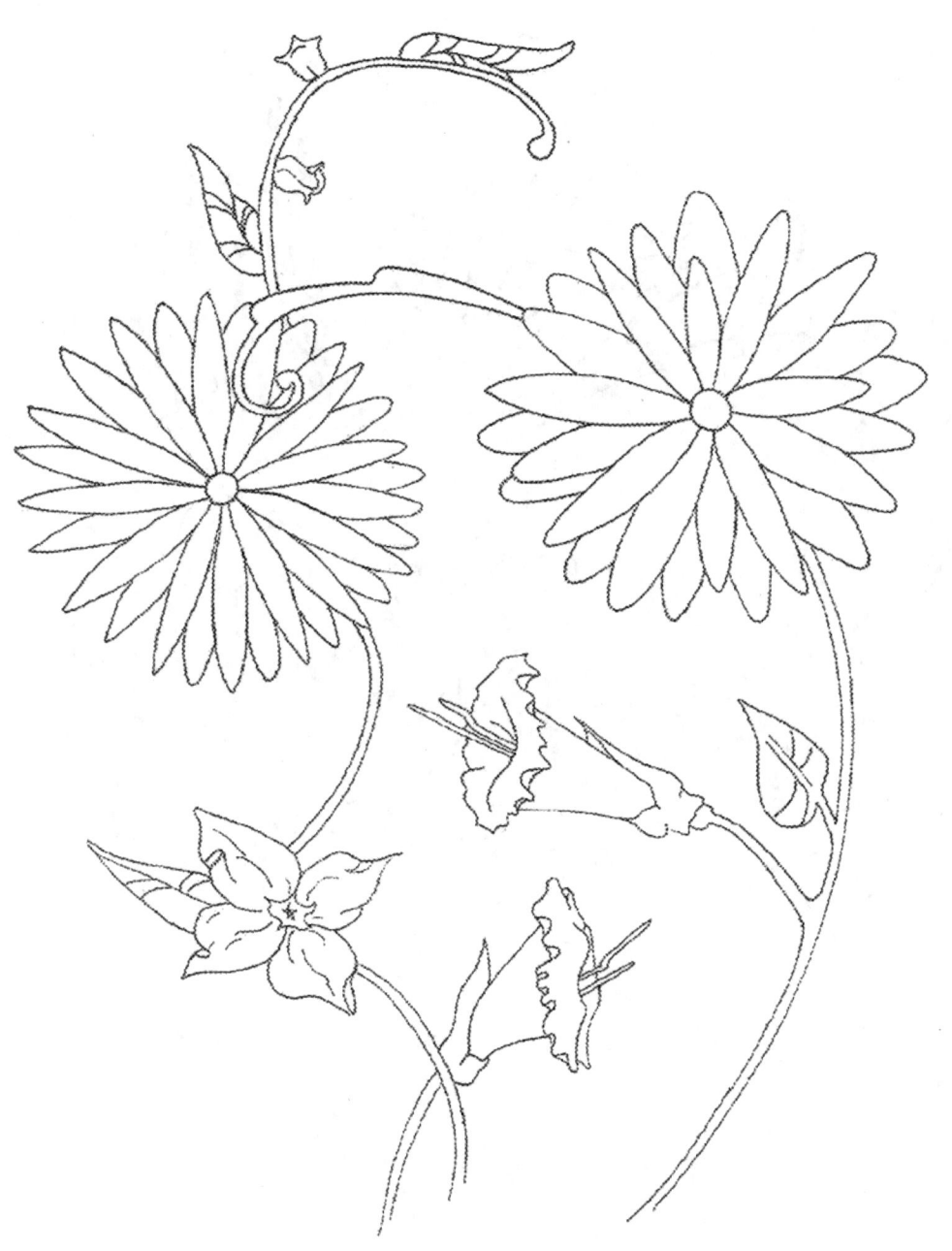

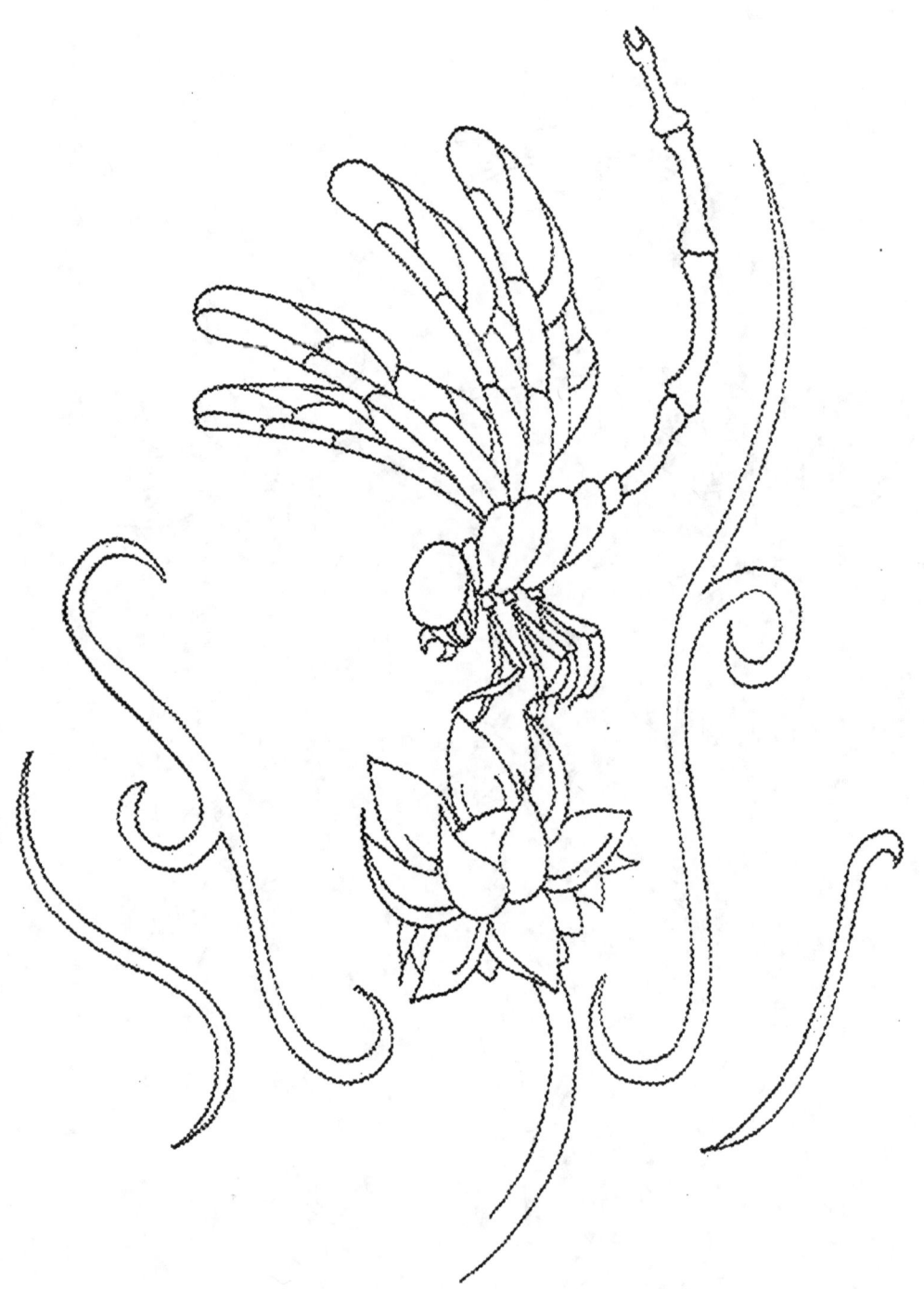

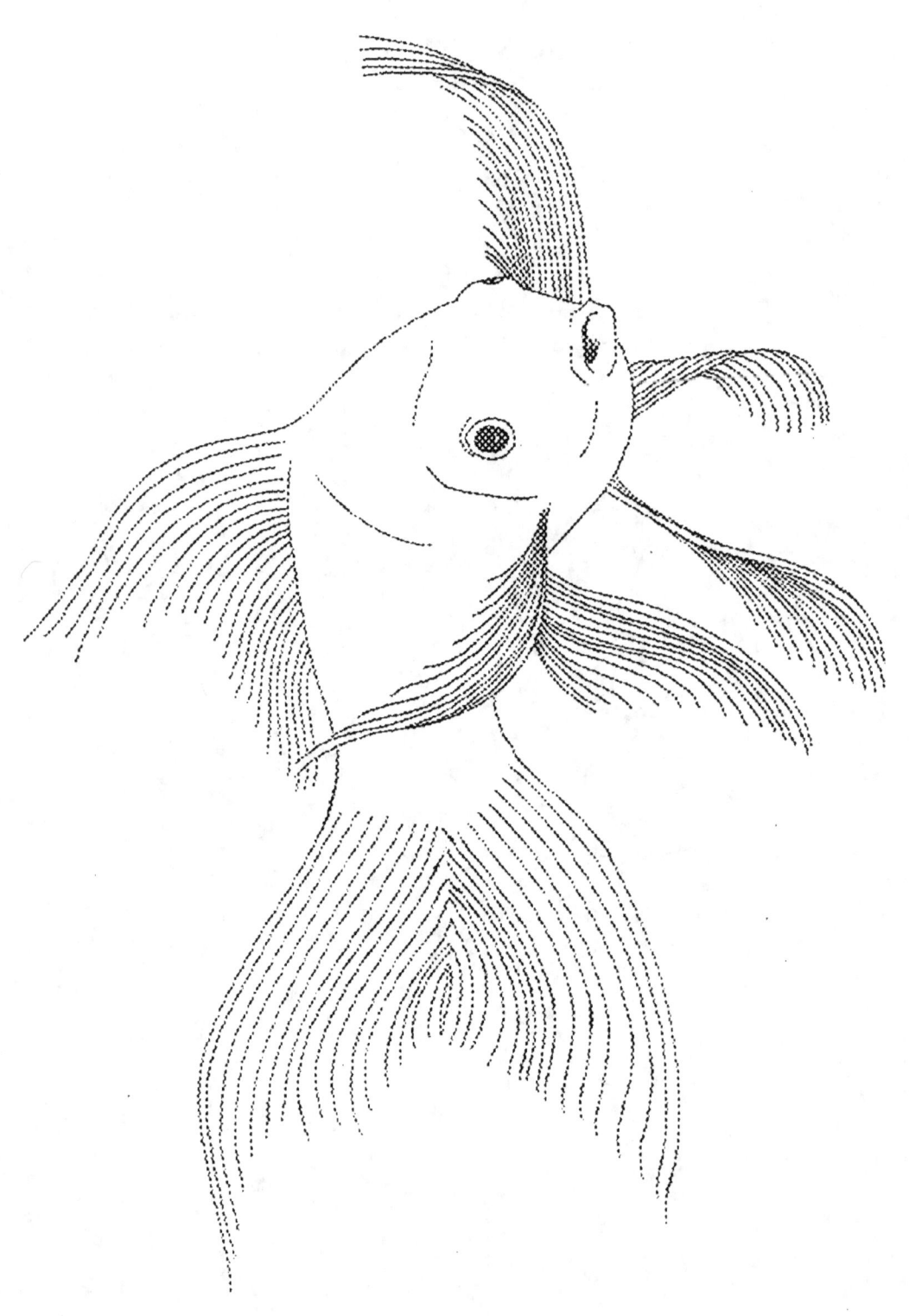

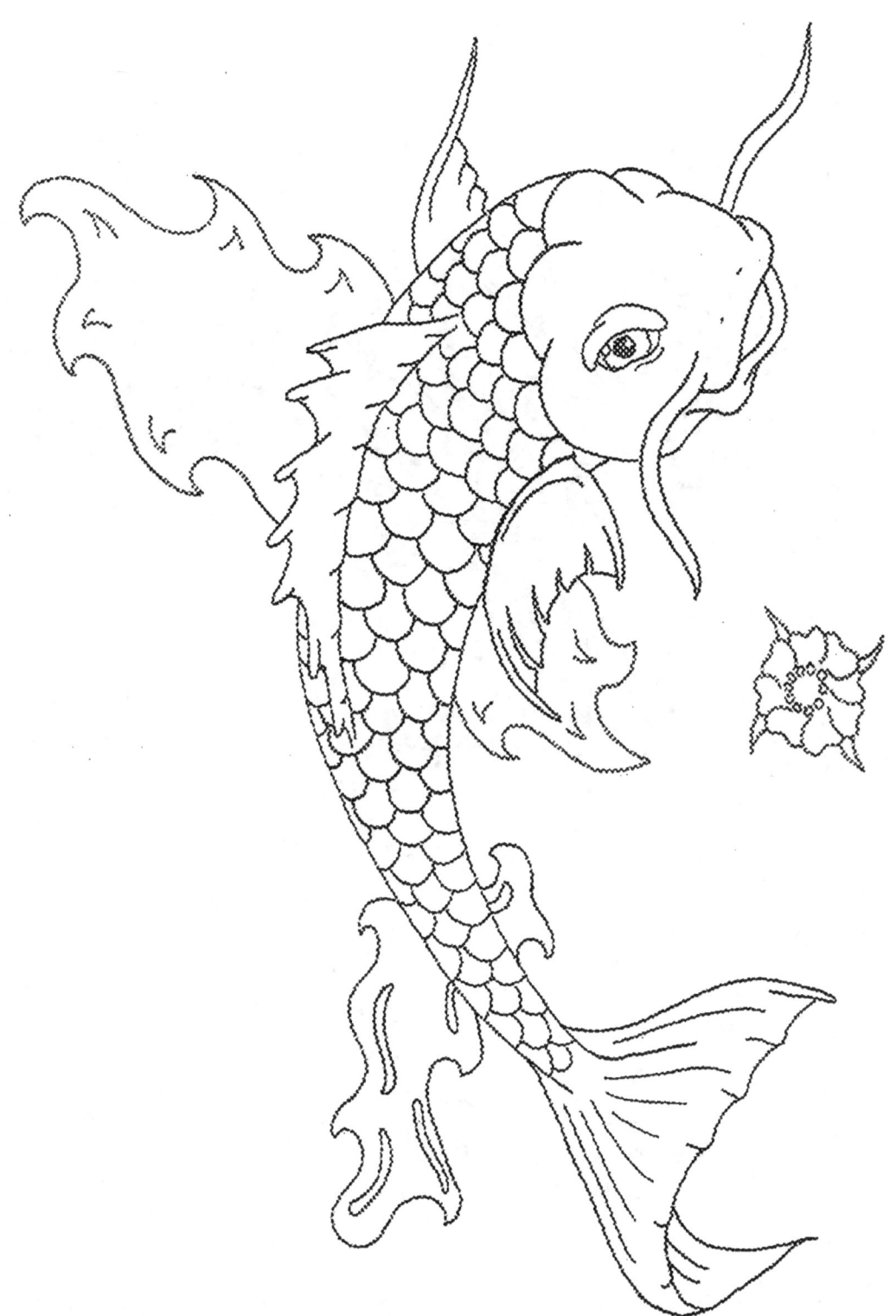

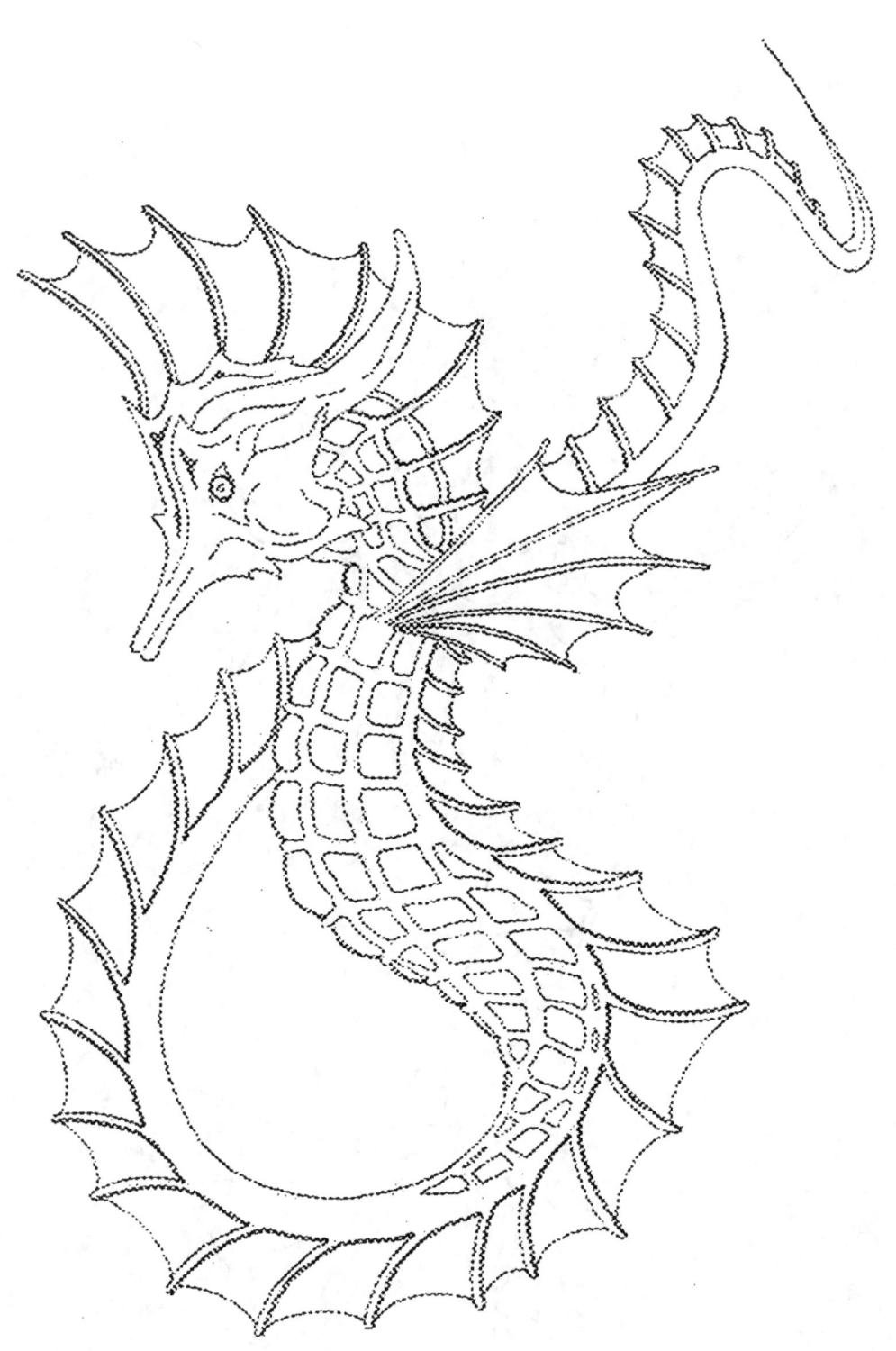

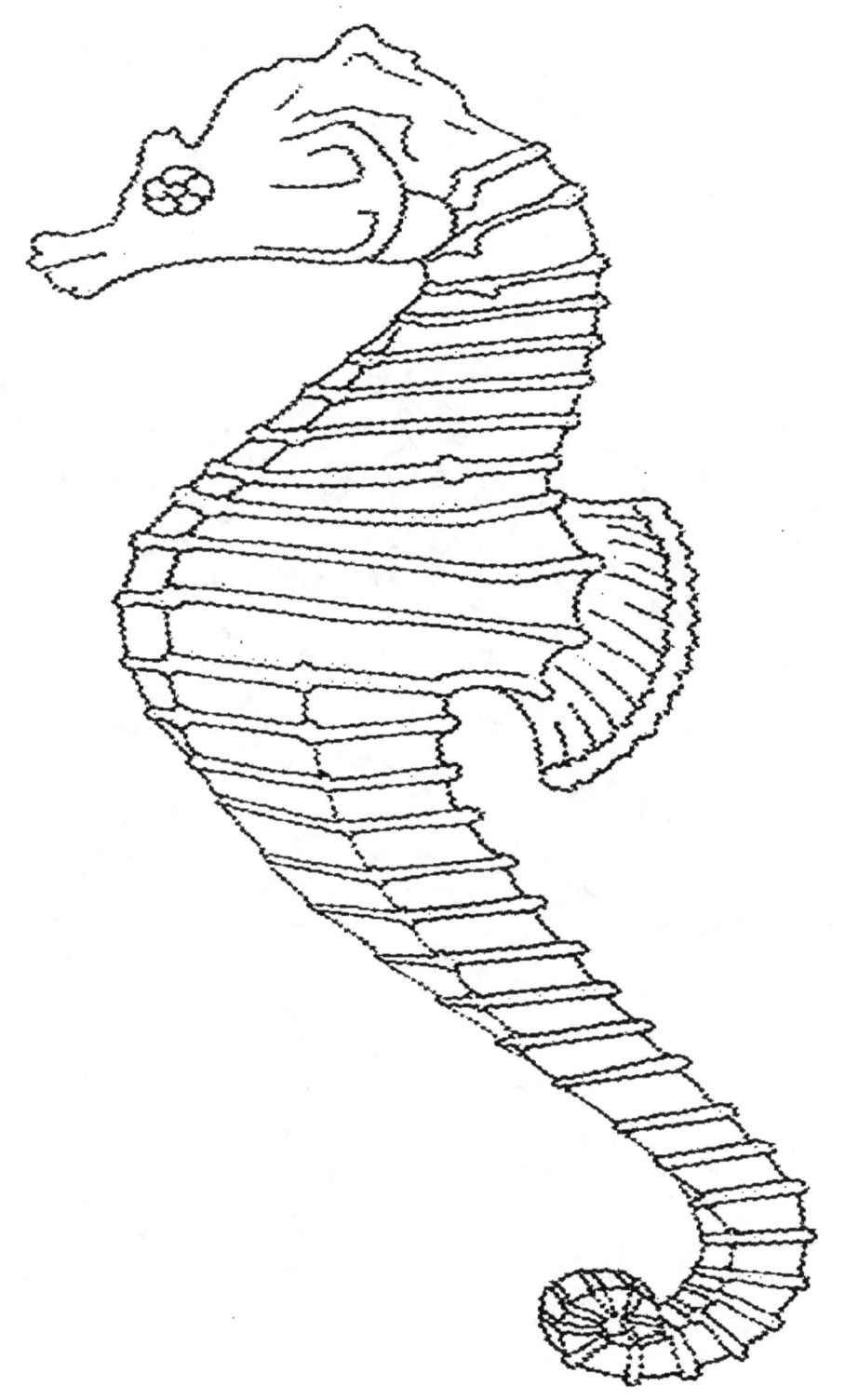

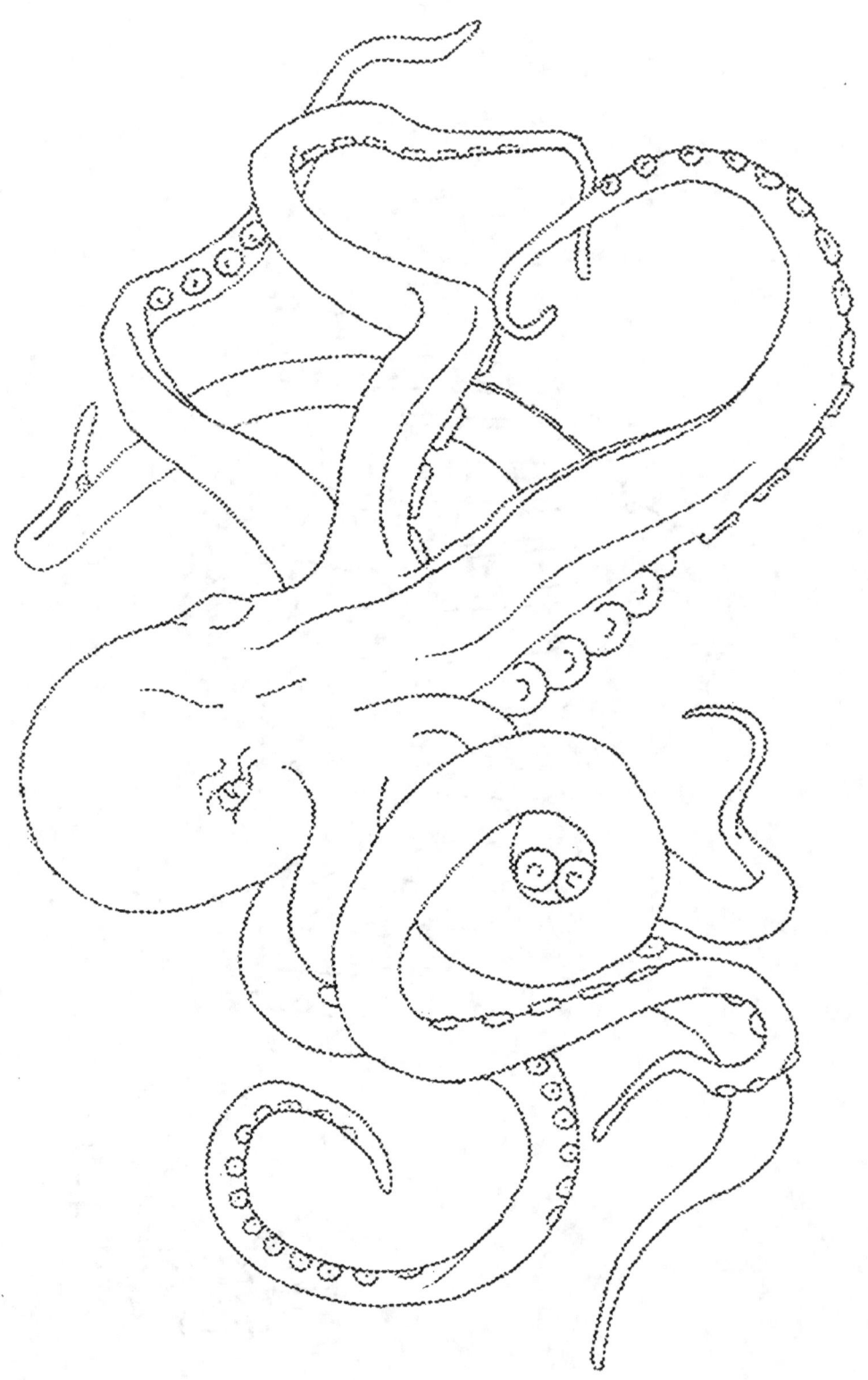

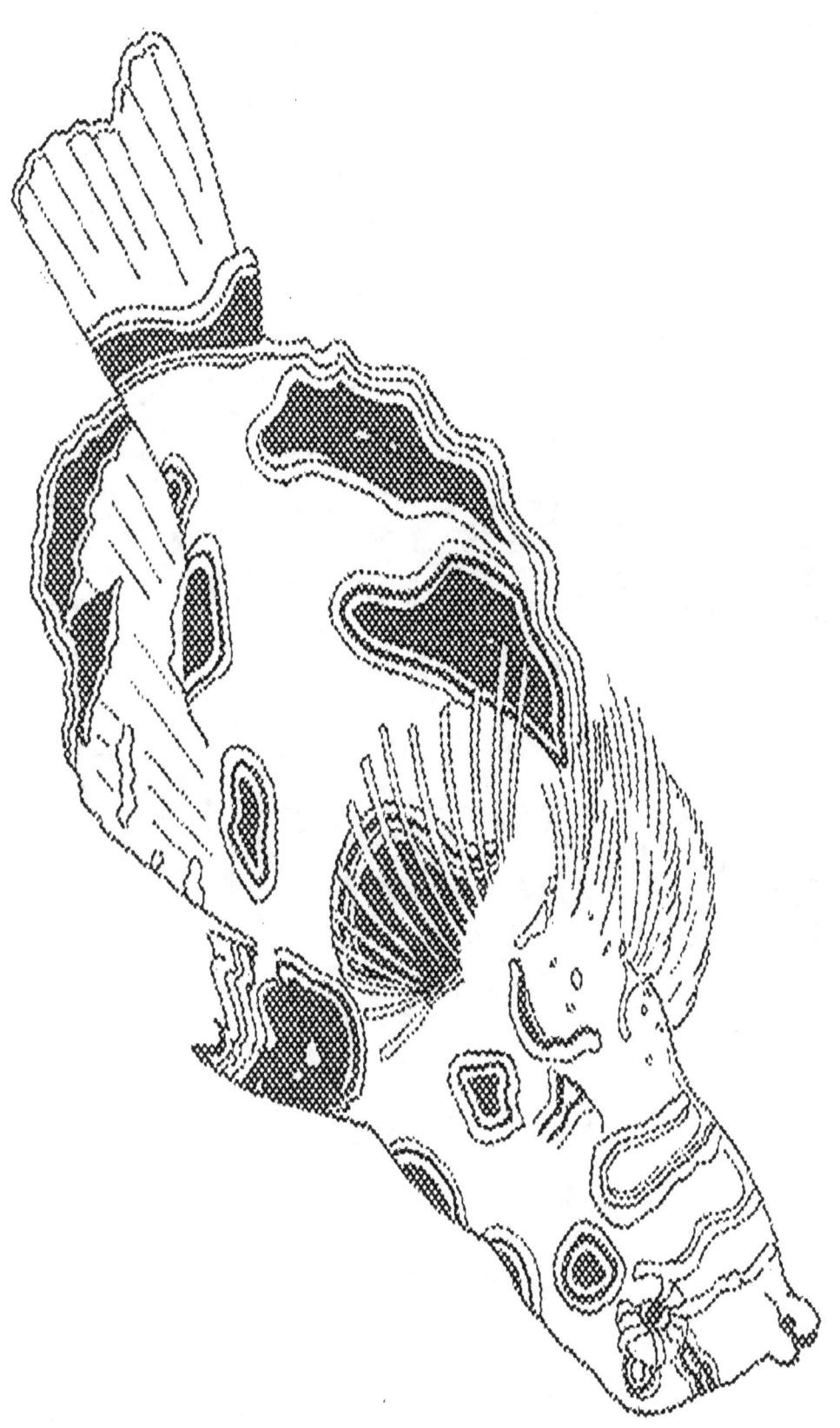

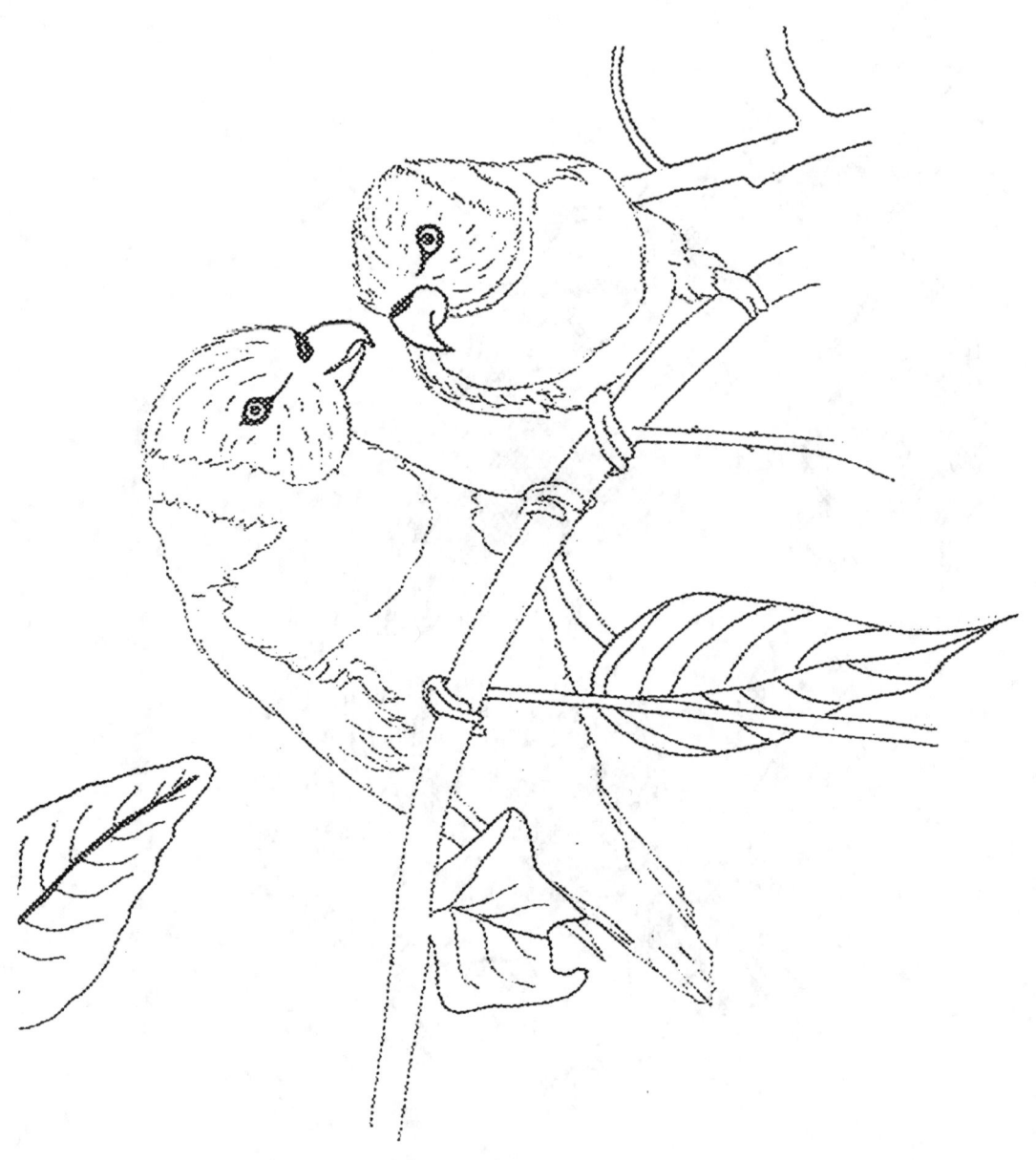

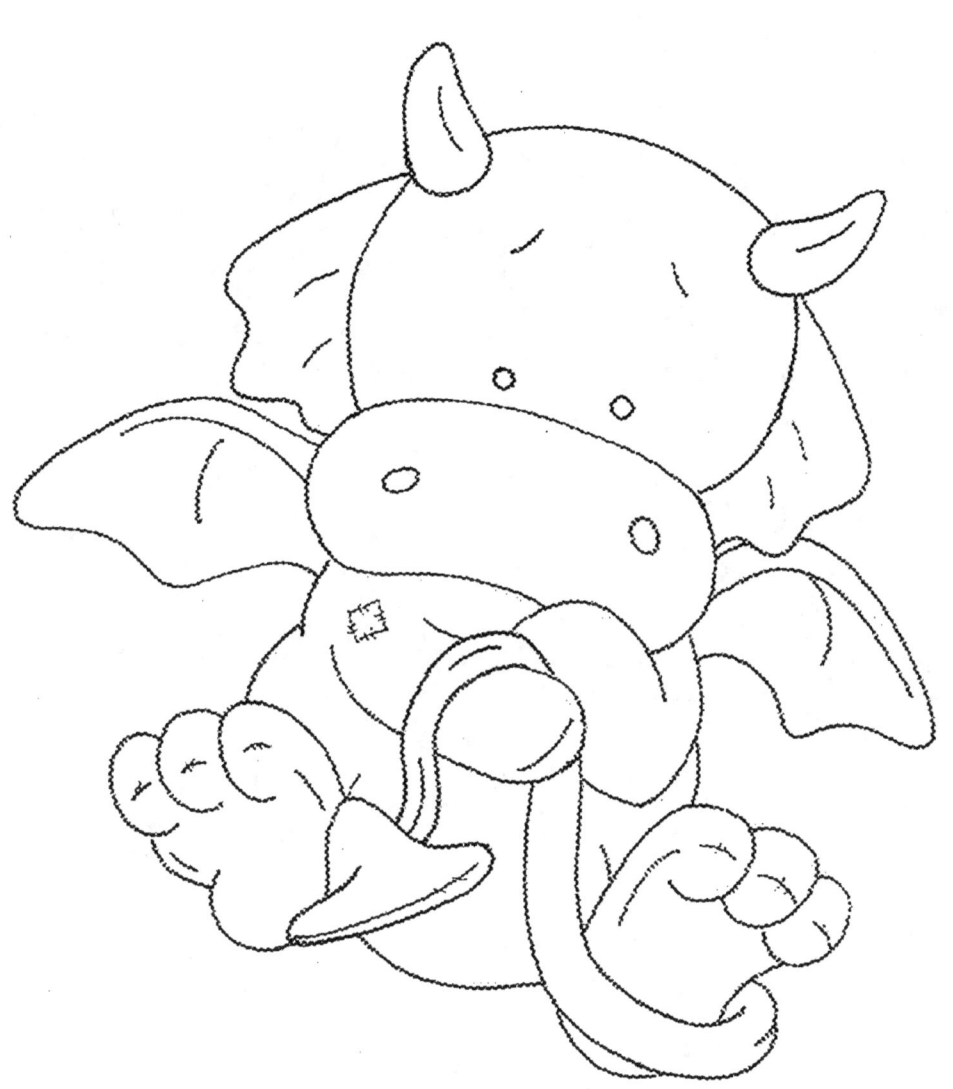

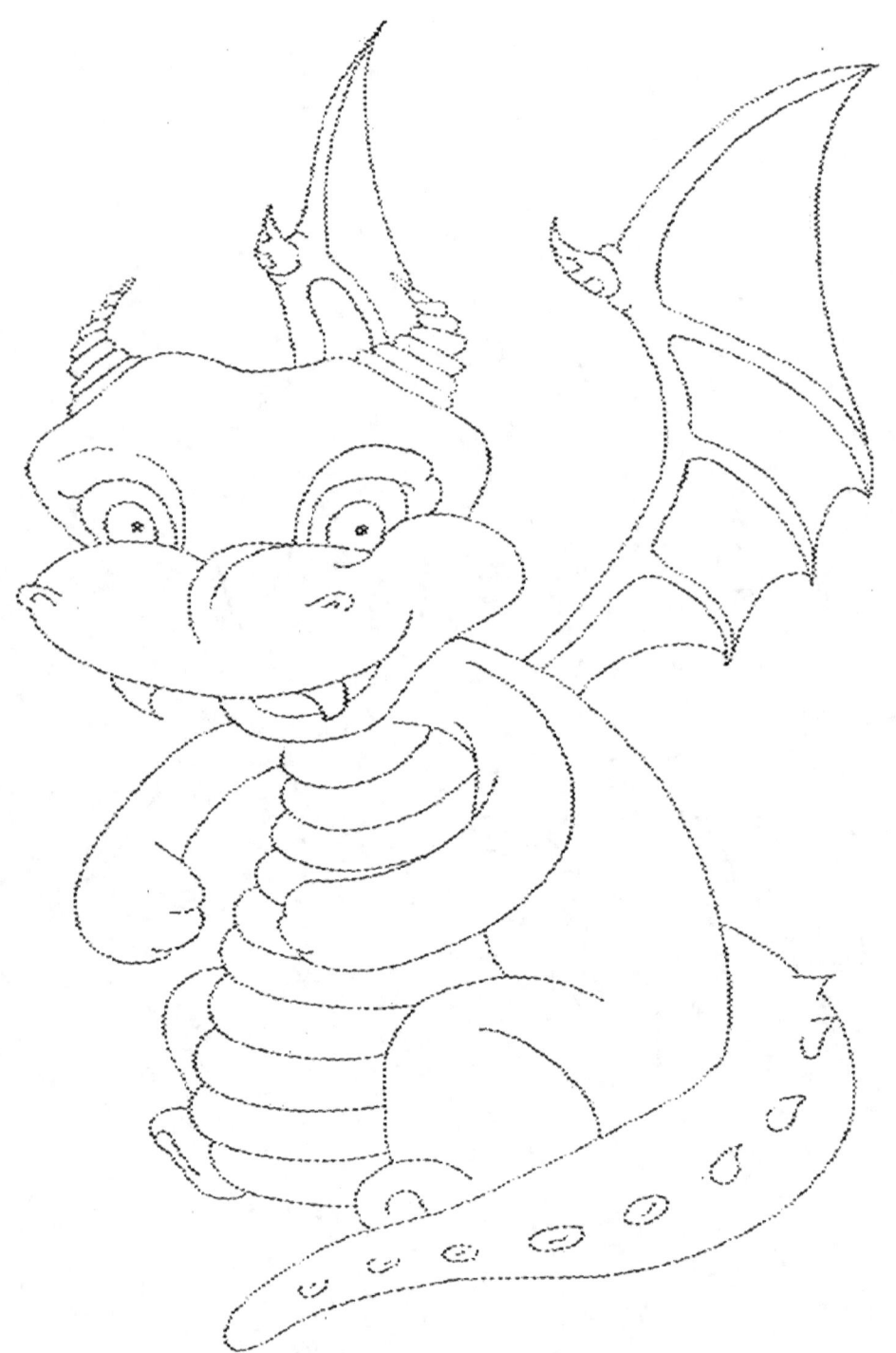

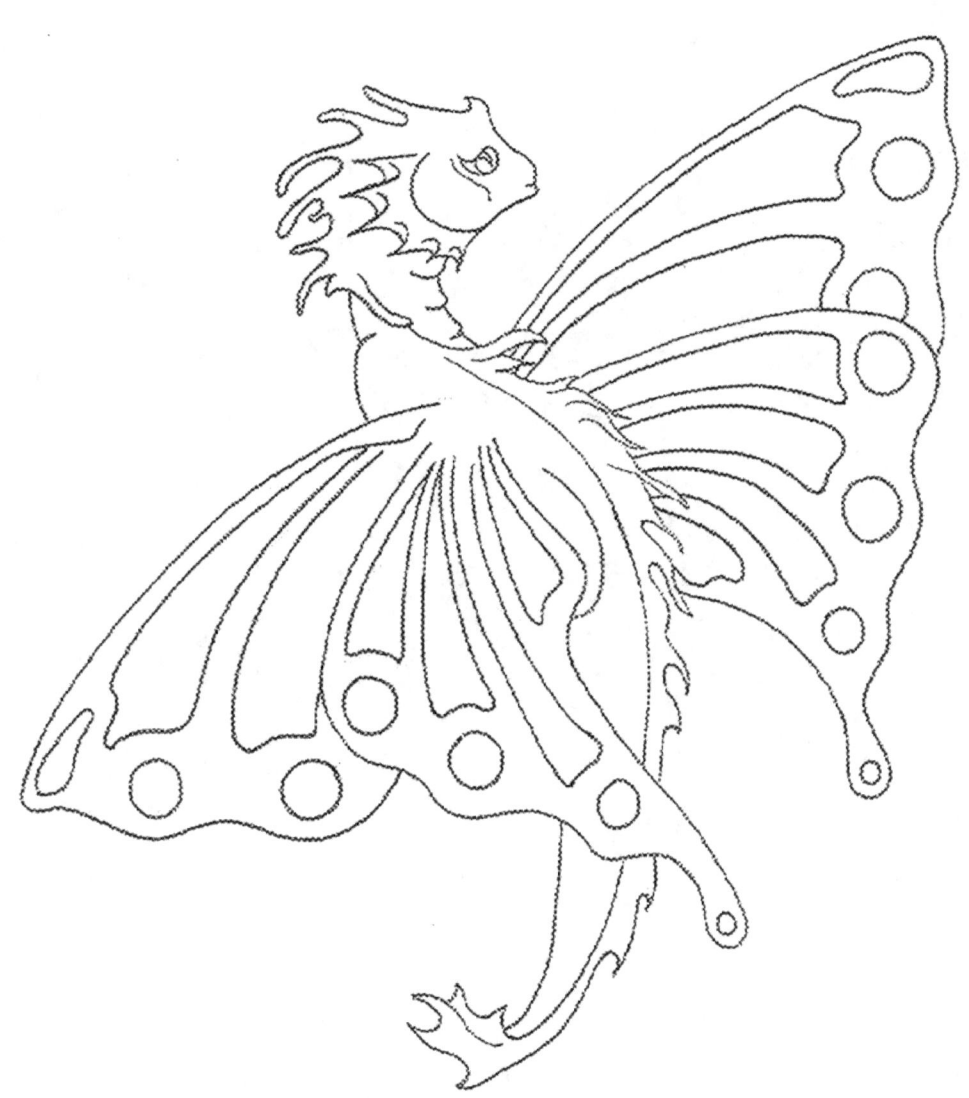

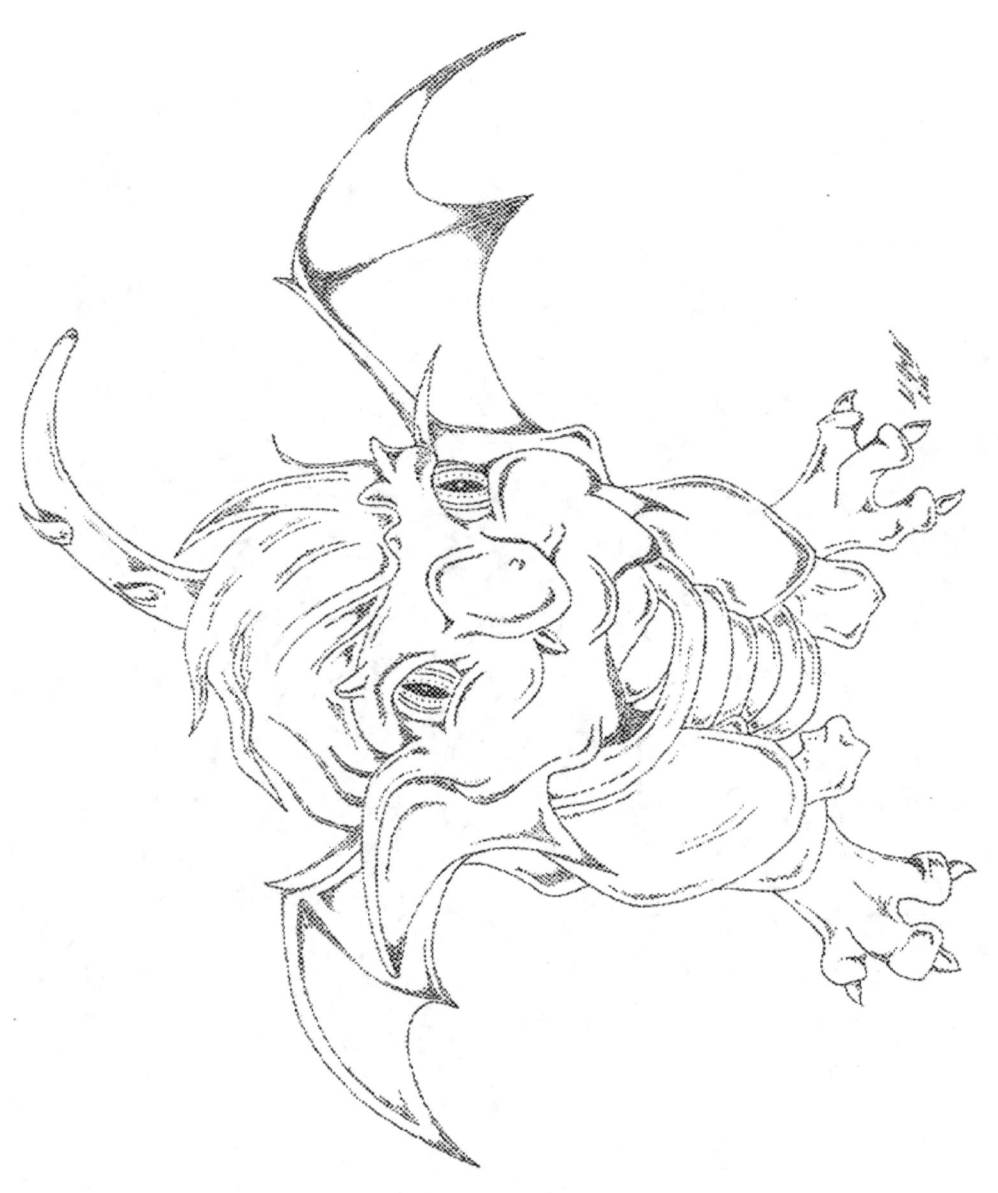

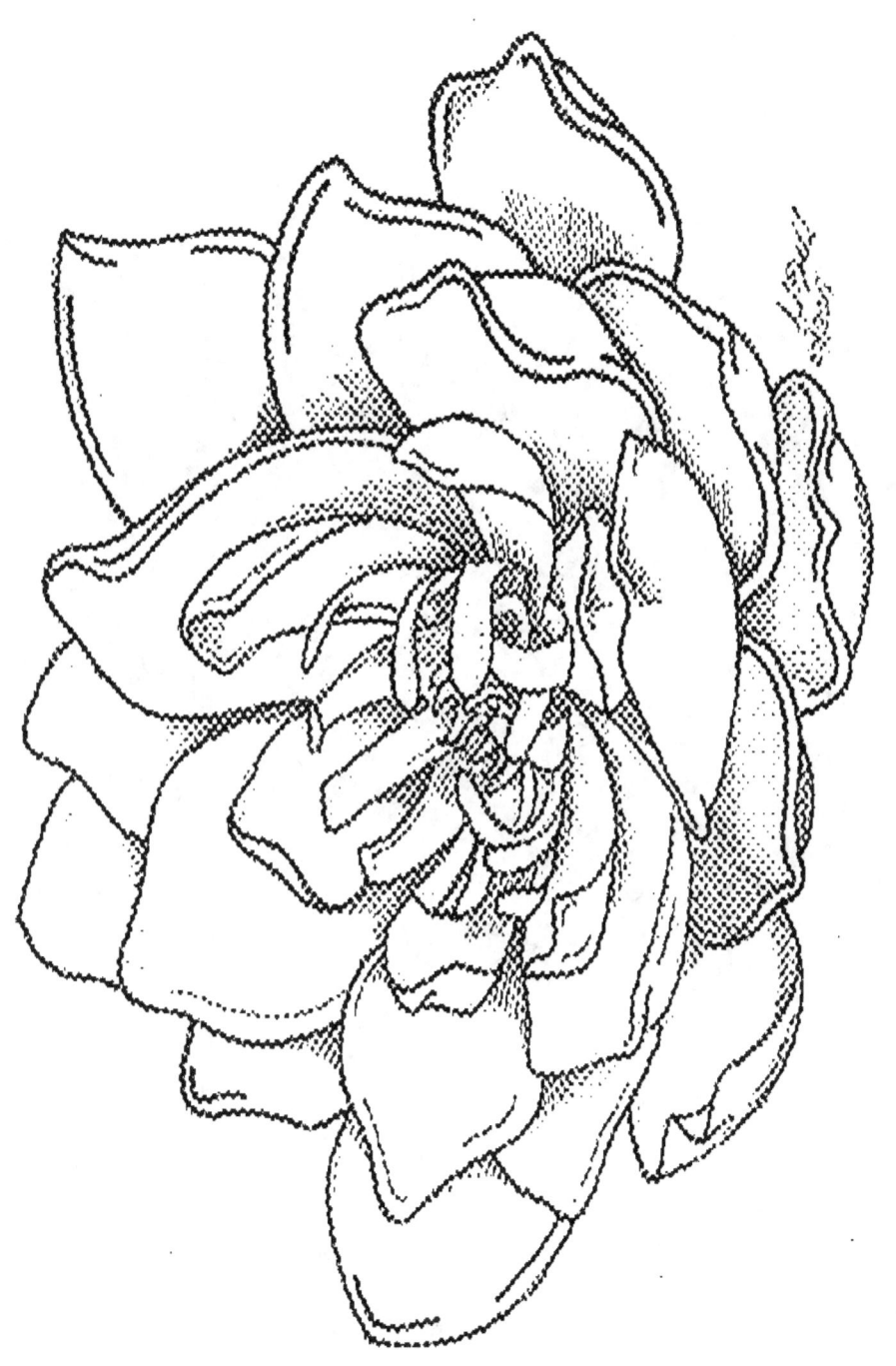

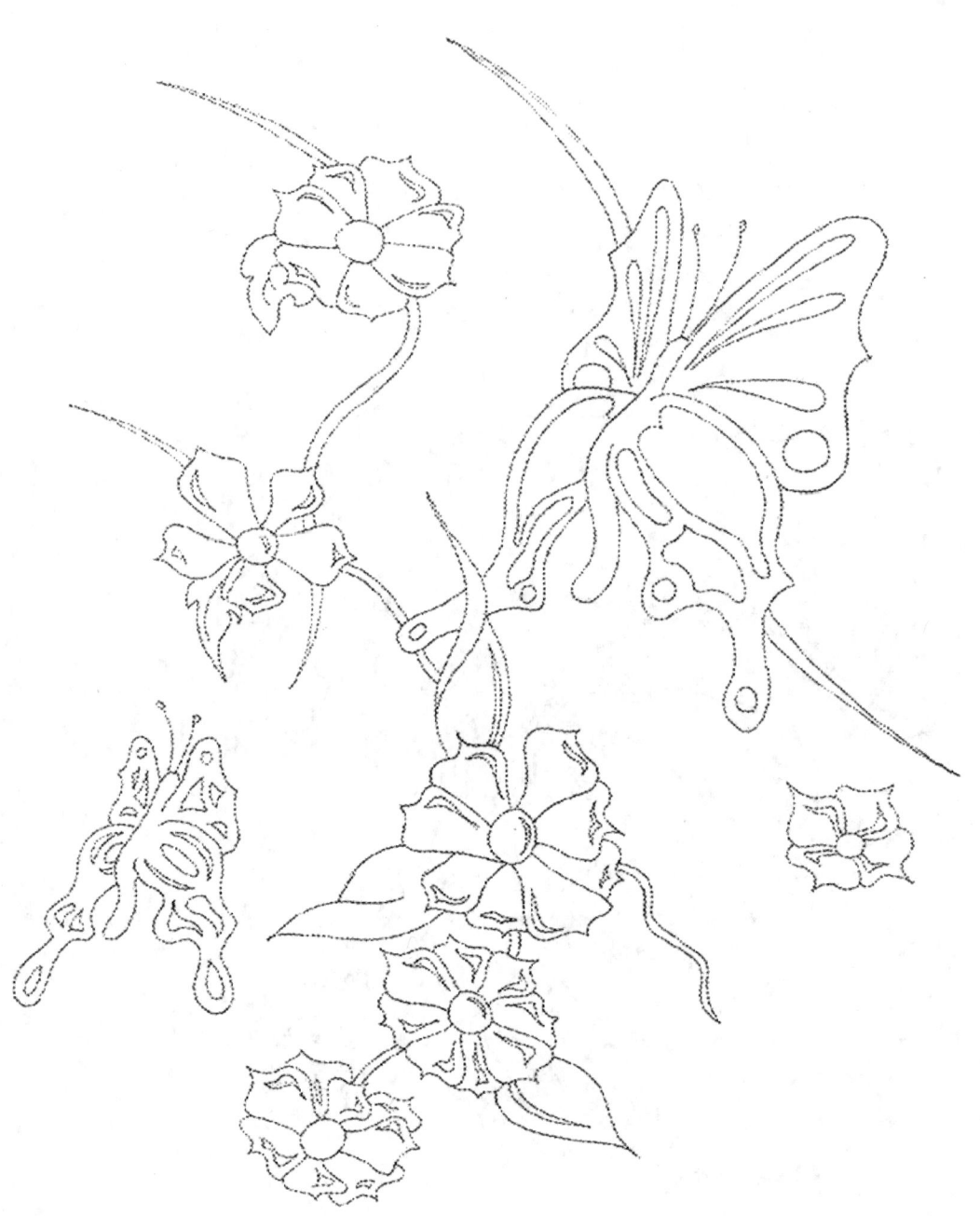

www.ingramcontent.com/pod-product-compliance
Lightning Source LLC
Chambersburg PA
CBHW082305200526
45168CB00018B/3412